A myth from Ancient Greece

Susan Gates

Illustrated by
Carlos Lara

CONTENTS

Dear Reader,

The story of Helen and the Trojan War is ancient. It has adventure, monsters, nail-biting suspense, heroic deeds and loads of action. It has gods who never stop plotting and taking sides.

Much of the story is fiction, but some of it is based on real events. The city of Troy really existed and there was a war between Trojans and Greeks. But never mind what's fiction and what's fact. The main thing is, it's a terrific story!

Susan Gates

Chapter 1
Achilles' revenge

My name is Karis. I am twelve years old. I am a serving maid to Helen of Troy. People say that she is the most beautiful woman in the world.

Every day I climb up to the great walls that surround the city of Troy. I watch our Trojan soldiers fighting the Greeks on the plain below. Then I go back and give my mistress news of the war.

Helen can never come to the walls now. Too many people hate her. The Greek soldiers hate her because she left her husband, Menelaus, the King of Sparta and leader of the Greeks. Ten years ago, Paris, the son of our King Priam, went to visit Menelaus. Menelaus was kind to Paris and gave him many gifts. But Paris repaid him by taking his wife, Helen. Helen and Paris ran away together to Troy, and have lived here ever since.

But then an army of Greek soldiers came to seek revenge for the insult to King Menelaus. They camped outside our walls, fighting our Trojan soldiers and trying to destroy our city.

The Trojan people hate my mistress too. At first they welcomed her. They were dazzled by her beauty. But this war has gone on for ten long years. Everyone is weary and hungry. Many brave Trojans have been killed. The people blame Helen for all their misery.

Today, as I rush through the streets, a

woman recognises me.

'There goes one of Helen's serving maids,' she cries, pointing her finger.

'How can you wait on that wicked Greek woman?' she hisses. 'This war is all her fault!'

I want to shout back, 'No, it isn't!' I heard King Priam say that Helen was just an excuse. He said that the Greeks always wanted a war with Troy, so they could steal our city's gold and riches.

But I know the woman won't listen. I pull the hood of my cloak over my head and hurry away.

Up on Troy's high walls, I gaze out over the wide, windy plain. Beyond it is the beach where the Greeks have pulled up their ships. There is a crowd of huts and tents. It is the camp where the Greek soldiers live. They say there are ten thousand of them.

Beyond the Greek camp is the blue sea.

Poseidon, the sea god, lives there with sea monsters and beautiful sea nymphs.

A Trojan sentry comes clanking up, carrying his spear. Some sentries chase me away but this one is always friendly.

'Here again, Karis?' he grins. 'There is no fighting yet. Those lazy Greek soldiers are still in bed.'

I shiver. The plain is empty now but I know that soon it will be a whirling, screaming chaos of chariots and horses and men fighting. I hate watching it. But I have to. My mistress depends on me, to bring her news.

A few days ago I saw a dreadful tragedy. Hector was killed.

Hector was Paris' eldest brother. He was also the greatest of our Trojan warriors. All us Trojans are in despair. People are wailing, 'What shall we do now Hector is dead? Who will lead our army?'

Hector was killed by Achilles, that mighty Greek warrior. Everyone in Troy knows and fears Achilles. People tremble when they hear his name. During battle, Hector had killed Achilles' best friend. Achilles wanted revenge. He came looking for Hector to challenge him to a fight to the death.

Achilles came raging up to the walls of Troy. He was in a terrible fury. His chariot wheels

were splashed with blood. Soldiers ran
shrieking from him in fear.

He bellowed, 'Hector, come out and fight!'

Achilles' father is mortal. But they say his mother is a sea goddess. They say that when he was born, she dipped him in the sacred river Styx so no weapons could harm him. His armour was made in heaven. When you see Achilles on the battlefield you can believe all that. His armour glitters like a hundred golden suns. Spears fly harmlessly past him.

Even Hector, Troy's greatest hero, trembled as he came out of Troy city to fight the mighty Achilles. For a few minutes a mist came down and hid him. People said it was the gods, trying to help him. But it was no use. Even the gods couldn't save Hector. When the mist cleared Achilles, running as fast as a deer, chased him. Then he killed him with his spear.

• *Styx:* (say) 'stiks'.

'Will Achilles come out to fight today?' I ask the friendly sentry.

He gives a grim smile. 'Look over there, Karis,' he says, pointing towards the Greek camp.

I see Greek soldiers marching out onto the plain. They are screaming war cries, clattering their spears against their shields. Out in front, I see something bobbing about, like a spray of bright red blood.

'That is the crest of Achilles' helmet,' says the sentry. 'Whenever he's with the Trojans they fight like wolves! Achilles is half god, half man. How can anyone kill him?'

Below me, I hear the clash of the main gates into Troy city. They are opening to let our soldiers out. The two armies march towards each other.

Then the fighting starts.

Chapter 2

Paris the hero

A short time later, I
am racing through the
corridors of Helen's
palace. The walls,
painted with red and
green flowers, flash past
me. I almost slip on the
gleaming stone floors.
I rush into my mistress'
chamber. I am so
breathless I can only blurt
out one word: 'News!'

My mistress has been
sewing her great tapestry,
which tells of the
glorious history of Troy.
She springs up from
her stool.

'Has Paris been killed?' she whispers, her face white with horror.

'No, mistress!' I manage to gasp. 'Paris is alive. He is a hero! He has just killed Achilles!'

'Achilles?' says Helen as if she can hardly believe it.

'Paris fired an arrow at Achilles,' I tell her. 'It struck him in the heel.'

'In the heel?' says my mistress, amazed. 'That killed the mighty Achilles?'

'Yes,' I nod, although I can hardly believe it either.

His friends tried frantically to help him. But it was hopeless.

Helen sits down again on her stool. I am still trembling with shock and excitement. 'Sit down beside me,' says my mistress. She strokes my hair, to make me calm.

Helen has always been kind to me. Most Trojans hate my mistress and I should hate her too. My father was killed in the war. Then my mother died soon after, of sickness, or a broken heart. I was all alone. Helen gave me work as her serving maid. She is so beautiful, like a goddess walking amongst us.

My mistress seems deep in thought. 'I can guess why Achilles died,' she says, suddenly. 'Perhaps, when his mother dipped him in the Styx, she held him by one heel. So that heel was his one weak spot. The only place he could be wounded.'

My mistress is wise, as well as beautiful.

'Perhaps the god Apollo helped Paris to kill Achilles,' murmurs my mistress. 'Perhaps he guided the arrow.'

Apollo, the sun god, has always been a friend to us Trojans.

Suddenly, we hear armour clashing and feet tramping in the corridor. We both leap up. Paris comes bursting into the room. His armour is covered in dust and dirt. I scurry into a corner.

'I, Paris, have killed the mighty Achilles!' he boasts to Helen.

'We must thank Apollo,' says my mistress.

'Apollo?' Paris crows. 'I did this alone. I didn't need Apollo's help!'

Chapter 3
The wooden horse

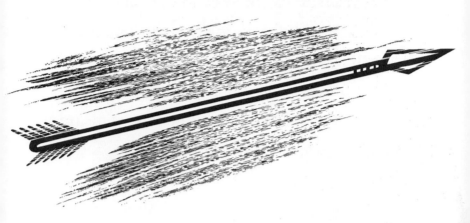

When the mighty Achilles was killed by Paris, we all thought Troy was saved. But then a terrible thing happened. Paris himself was killed – by a poisoned arrow.

Some say the gods had a part in it because Paris was too proud. Since killing Achilles he boasted, 'I'm a greater hero than my brother Hector!' Some say the arrow was dipped in the blood of the Hydra, a many-headed monster, and that's why Paris died so quickly, despite all our doctors' skills.

• *Hydra:* (say) 'hy-druh'. **19**

After Paris died, I thought my mistress would go mad with grief. Helen tore her gown and wailed and cried. She did not eat or speak for days. But this morning she said, 'Karis, bring me some bread and wine.'

Then she said, 'Bring me news of the war.'

'Yes mistress!' I ran off immediately, pleased that my mistress needed me.

So here I am, up on the walls again. It's still early. The sun is just coming up. Slowly, the mists clear from the plain.

And I can't believe my eyes!

'There's a big wooden horse down there!' I cry out, to my friendly sentry.

Then we both look beyond the horse.

'The Greeks have gone!' gasps the sentry.

It's true. The beach
is completely empty.
During the night the
Greeks have packed their
tents and slipped away
in their ships.

Another sentry comes
running up. He shakes
his spear in the air in
triumph. 'The Greeks
have given up! We've
won the war!'

The good news
spreads through Troy,
as fast as flying arrows.
'The Greeks have gone!'
People shout it from the
tops of our highest towers.

But why did they go? Everyone has their own explanation.

'It's because the gods have turned against them.'

'It's because their hero, Achilles, is dead.'

I should be rushing to tell my mistress. But somehow, I can't tear my eyes away from that strange wooden horse. It's enormous, as tall as four men. It stands there silent, before the city gates. As if it is waiting for something.

Then the huge gates are flung open. Men, women and children pour out onto the plain. I hear the guards shouting, 'Make way for King Priam!'

The old King comes tottering out from the city with Queen Hecuba. My mistress, Helen, is with them! She walks through the gates, in her finest robes, her head held high.

I go dashing down the stone steps to join my mistress.

I stand proudly beside Helen. I glare
defiantly at the crowd as if to say, 'Don't you
dare call my mistress rude names!' But no one
does. They're all too excited and joyful. 'Troy is
free!' they are shouting. 'The war is over!'

Many people surround the mysterious
wooden horse.

Someone says, 'The Greeks must have left it.'
Someone else says, 'It's a gift from the gods.'

People are bowing down to it. Some put garlands of flowers at its feet.

But Laocoön, a priest, is suspicious. He walks out of the crowd.

'I don't trust the Greeks,' he shouts, loudly. 'What if this horse is a trick? We should break it open!'

He hurls his spear at the horse.
The spear sticks in its wooden side
and quivers.

Just at that moment, some of our
soldiers arrive from the beach. They're
dragging a captive with them.

'Great King, the Greeks have all
sailed away,' they tell Priam. 'But they
left this one behind.'

The captive falls on his knees before Priam.

'My name is Sinon,' he tells us. 'And although I'm a Greek, all Greeks are my enemies now. They wanted to sacrifice me to Apollo. Just so they had fair winds for their ships. That old fool, Calchas, the soothsayer, who says he can see into the future, told them to do it. But I escaped. Now I haven't a friend in the world. Unless you Trojans take pity on me.'

Sinon starts crying like a baby. He clasps the King's knees, begging for mercy.

King Priam, feeling sorry for the poor man, says, 'Set him free!' Then he tells Sinon, 'In return, you must tell us all you know about this wooden horse.'

'Gladly!' says Sinon. 'The Greeks built it. It's a gift to the goddess Athene, so she'll grant them a safe journey home. It was the idea of Odysseus, the great Greek hero.'

'That's just like him!' someone shouts. Odysseus is well known for being clever.

• *Calchas:* (say) 'kal-kuss'. • *Athene:* (say) 'uh-theen-uh'.
• *Odysseus:* (say) 'uh-diss-ee-oos'.

'It is indeed a magnificent offering,' says old King Priam.

'It reaches almost to the sun!' cries a little boy, gazing upwards, his eyes bright with wonder.

'Ahhh,' says Sinon, smiling at the boy. 'There's a reason for the horse's great height. It's so it won't go through your city gates. Calchas told us that once the horse is inside your city, Athene will protect Troy forever.'

A woman starts shouting, 'Take the horse inside the city! Then Athene will always protect us.'

'An excellent idea!' agrees Sinon. Then he glares at Laocoön, whose spear is still stuck in the horse's side. 'But no one must damage the horse. Or try to break it open. For then Athene will be angry. She will destroy your city, instead of protecting it.'

All the listeners believe him. They know that if a god or goddess gets angry, they can take terrible vengeance. From Mount Olympus, where they live, they can send down plagues, or earthquakes. They can destroy entire armies or a whole city.

But Laocoön is still suspicious. He strides up to the horse, rips his spear out of the wood and spies through the hole it made. 'The horse is hollow inside!' he says.

'Come away, you foolish old man,' Sinon warns. 'You will anger Athene.'

Then, as if to prove his words true, an awful thing happens.

Someone points out to sea. 'Look at the monsters!'

Two sea serpents rear up from the blue water. They swim towards the shore, their scaly heads and snake-like necks rising above the waves. They have blood red crests and blazing eyes. Their tongues flicker from their hissing mouths! Now they are slithering up the beach!

People are panicking, shrieking, 'Run for your lives!'

I want to run too but my mistress Helen holds my arms. 'Stay here,' she commands. 'Our guards will protect us.'

The guards begin to form a circle round the royal family, facing outwards, their spears at the ready.

But the serpents aren't interested in the royal
family. They slither past them and straight up
to Laocoön, who is too frozen with fear to run.

The serpents seize Laocoön. It is terrible to see. The serpents tighten their grip and squeeze. Laocoön is trying to stab the writhing monsters. They wind their coils more tightly around him! Their black venom drenches his hair. Laocoön struggles desperately, trying to tear their knots apart.

I close my eyes because I can't bear to look anymore. When I open them again the two serpents are gliding away from Laocoön's

lifeless body. They go
through the city gates
into the city. When they
reach Athene's temple
they disappear into
a hole in the ground
beside her statue.

The Trojan people
stare after them.
They are shocked and
trembling, horror on
every face.

Some say, 'That is
Athene's punishment
for damaging her horse.'

Others say, 'Quick, take the horse into Troy, so the goddess won't punish anyone else!'

Frantically, everyone sets to work. They put rollers under the horse and tie ropes around its neck. Even the smallest child pulls their hardest. I join in too, tugging a rope.

'Careful,' people warn each other. 'Don't damage Athene's horse.'

Will it go through the city gates? People hold their breath. But it just fits.

'Ha ha,' laughs someone. 'So much for clever Odysseus! He should have made it taller!'

People are cheering as it rocks through the gates.

But what's that clanging sound? It seems to come from inside the horse.

I listen again. I can't hear anything now.

'You must have imagined it, Karis,' I tell myself.

Chapter 4
The fall of Troy

I am sitting with my mistress Helen, in
her palace.

It's many hours since we dragged the wooden
horse into our city.

Outside, people are having a big party.
Everyone is feasting and dancing.

But my mistress, Helen, isn't celebrating.

'Aren't you happy, mistress?' I ask her. 'The Greeks have gone. The war is over. Troy can never fall, now the wooden horse is inside our walls. Didn't you hear Sinon tell us so?'

Helen strokes my hair.

'I wish I could believe Sinon's words,' she says.

'Do you think he was lying?' I ask.

My mistress frowns. 'I don't know,' she answers. 'But there's something about that man I don't trust.' She shivers, then tries to smile. 'But perhaps I am just too suspicious.'

As time passes the city grows silent. Everyone must be sound asleep, tired after food and dancing.

'Time for you to go to bed, Karis,' says my mistress, seeing me give a great yawn.

I'm stumbling to my bed when I suddenly think of my friendly sentry. He must be cold and lonely up there on the walls. Perhaps he'd like some food too.

Soon, I'm climbing up to the walls with some honey cakes.

It's still dark. But then the moon sails out from behind a cloud.

By its silvery light I can see there are no sentries here.

The walls are empty.

Then I realise why. 'You're so silly, Karis,' I tell myself, chuckling. 'Why do we need sentries, now the Greeks have gone away?'

But wait, I can see someone in the shadows. They seem to be sneaking around. I crouch down so I can't be seen. Then a red flame flares out. The person has lit a torch. They stand up. And by the torch's light I see who it is.

'Sinon,' I whisper.

He waves the torch to and fro. From the darkness, far out at sea, comes an answering signal.

What is he up to? Perhaps my mistress was right not to trust him.

Sinon pads down the stone steps.

I follow, keeping out of sight. There are no guards to stop or challenge him. They are all asleep and snoring.

Sinon creeps to the wooden horse. He ducks under its belly.

'What's he doing?' I ask myself.

Then I give a horrified gasp. He's opening a secret door! Greek warriors, fully armed, slide out of the horse. One is Odysseus himself. I recognise his helmet crest. The soldiers run towards the city gates.

And at last I understand.

'The wooden horse was a trick!' I whisper.

Poor Laocoön was right. The Greeks used it to get inside our city. And now they are rushing to open the city gates to let in the rest of the army.

They never
really went away.
Their ships just
sailed out of
sight and waited
for Sinon's signal.
Now they are sailing
back. At this very moment,
they are probably landing their
soldiers on our beach.

I must warn my mistress. The Greeks will
take her prisoner. Or even kill her.

Everything happens with horrible swiftness. By the time I've woken my mistress, I can hear screams and war cries and sounds of fighting in the streets outside. The Greek army is here already!

My mistress, Helen, is calm and courageous. 'Save yourself, Karis,' she commands.

'No!' I cry. 'I will never leave you!'

'Then let us try to escape together,' she says.

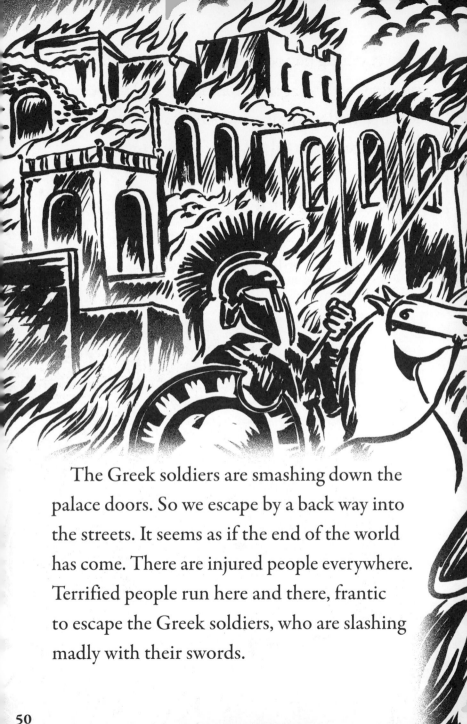

The Greek soldiers are smashing down the
palace doors. So we escape by a back way into
the streets. It seems as if the end of the world
has come. There are injured people everywhere.
Terrified people run here and there, frantic
to escape the Greek soldiers, who are slashing
madly with their swords.

In the background is a terrible roaring, like a great, raging monster. Troy is on fire. Black smoke hangs over the city. All our palaces and temples are burning.

A man with wild, staring eyes comes
rushing past us. 'They have killed Priam!' he is
shouting. 'They have killed our king!'

My mistress and I are nearly at the city gates.
She is wearing a hooded cloak, which hides
her face. No one has recognised her yet as the
beautiful Helen of Troy.

'If we can reach the beach,' she says, 'we might find a boat.'

I feel a tiny spark of hope inside me. Perhaps we really can escape!

Then, suddenly, someone yells, 'Stop!'

A tall figure steps out in front of us. He throws back Helen's hood.

'Don't you remember me, Helen?' he asks her. 'The husband you left behind in Sparta?'

'Menelaus!' gasps my mistress.

Menelaus turns to his soldiers and commands them, 'Put her in chains!'

Chapter 5
Return to Sparta

At first, when my mistress and I were captured, I feared for her life. But an amazing thing happened. Menelaus gradually lost his anger. After ten years, he still loved Helen, so he forgave her. He even said, 'You must come back to Sparta and be Queen again.'

My mistress asked, 'Karis, will you come with us to Sparta? You will be treated with kindness. You will have a new life.'

I said yes. I have never left Troy in my life. But now Troy is an empty ruin, all its beautiful buildings burned to the ground. The Trojan men are dead and the women and children taken as slaves. There is nothing left for me.

So now we are sailing away, on a Greek ship.
There are tears in my eyes as I gaze back at
my ruined city. I take one last sad look, then
turn away. The fresh sea breeze dries my tears.

Life moves on and I am already thinking,
'Perhaps I shall like Sparta, after all.'